The New Campfire COOKBOOK

Pie Iron Sandwiches and Kebabs

ANNE SCHAFFER

FOX CHAPEL
PUBLISHING

15

© 2023 by Anne Schaeffer and Fox Chapel Publishing Company, Inc., 903 Square Street, Mount Joy, PA 17552.

Recipe selection, design, and book design © Fox Chapel Publishing. Recipes and photographs © G&R Publishing DBA CQ Products.

ISBN 978-1-4971-0385-6

The Cataloging-in-Publication Data is on file with the Library of Congress.

To learn more about the other great books from Fox Chapel Publishing, or to find a retailer near you, call toll-free 800-457-9112 or visit us at *www.FoxChapelPublishing.com*.

We are always looking for talented authors. To submit an idea, please send a brief inquiry to acquisitions@foxchapelpublishing.com.

Printed in China
First printing

28

40

108

CONTENTS

46

55

35

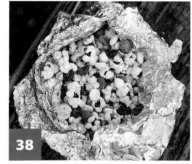

38

51

63

48

68

72

77

105

116

112

Sauces 104

Desserts 106

INTRODUCTION

One of the best ways to connect to nature, whether you're camping in the woods or relaxing in your backyard, is to cook your meal over a crackling fire. As you look out at the trees in front of you, the smell of smoke and cooking cheese and bread will be sure to warm your heart after a long day adventuring, exploring, and observing. In *The New Campfire Cookbook: Pie Iron Sandwiches and Kebabs*, you will find recipes for breakfast, lunch, dinner, and everything in between, full of delicious ingredients that you can prep, freeze, pack, and eat whenever you feel hungry. In this book, you will find stress-free, delicious, fun, and filling foods for any meal or appetite. Not only will you see delicious recipes for sandwiches, but also skewers, kebabs, and sauces. Enjoy flipping through over 100 options, choosing your favorites, and when it comes time to build that campfire, use the following handy helpful tips to keep your campfire cooking easy.

TIPS FOR COOKING AT CAMP

Remember to read through your chosen recipes beforehand and plan ahead for ways to make your life easier if you're cooking away from home.

- Pre-mix your dry ingredients, fillings, and spices and store them in labeled zippered plastic bags or airtight containers.
- Note which recipes have make-at-home options and prepare and pack those ahead of time.
- Buy shredded or sliced vegetables and cheese so you don't have to do that prepping yourself.
- Create a list of additional food items you might need for making pie iron sandwiches, kebabs, or sauces, like cooking spray, bread, or skewers.
- Finally, review the **Camp Cooking Tools You Might Need checklist** to be sure you've packed all the cooking and safety items you might need.

CAMP COOKING TOOLS YOU MIGHT NEED

- ☐ paper goods (paper towels, napkins)
- ☐ dish cloths and towels
- ☐ tableware— silverware, plates, bowls, and cups
- ☐ a first-aid kit
- ☐ leather gloves/oven mitts/potholders
- ☐ a whisk

- ☐ sharp knives
- ☐ a long, metal spatula
- ☐ long, metal tongs
- ☐ a long, metal meat fork
- ☐ measuring cups and spoons
- ☐ a can opener
- ☐ a pair of scissors
- ☐ a long lighter and matches

- ☐ a digital meat thermometer
- ☐ propane or charcoal
- ☐ dry wood, kindling wood, newspaper, and fire starters
- ☐ heavy-duty foil and foil pans
- ☐ a baking sheet
- ☐ skewers
- ☐ a pie iron

Above all, stay flexible and have fun. If you forgot something, you can improvise without worry! Pie iron meals can easily be turned into foil pack or skillet meals and seasonings and toppings can be adjusted based on what you have available. Your pie iron sandwiches can be as much as an adventure as the trip itself.

BUILDING THE PERFECT COOKING FIRE

First things first: you'll only get a nice cooking fire if you use the right kind of firewood. Use split logs since they produce the best heat and are easiest to ignite. Hard woods such as maple, walnut, oak, or apple are best; they burn slowly and produce wonderful cooking coals.

Pile up tinder in the cooking area; light with a match or lighter. When the tinder is burning well, place kindling loosely on top, adding more as needed. Once the kindling is burning nicely, carefully add split firewood, teepee-style, over the burning kindling.

When the flames die down, white hot coals remain. Use a metal fire poker or long stick to distribute the coals for cooking, as needed.

CAMPFIRE COOKING BASICS

Whatever method of cooking you choose—grill, foil, pie iron, skewer—remember to grease it before cooking. If camping with kids, adult supervision is essential! Only a few people can safely cook around a campfire at once, so campers should take turns, be nice, and avoid poking or chasing anyone with sharpened sticks or flaming marshmallows.

Foil Cooking

Heavy-duty foil is a camper's best friend. It has multiple uses and makes for easy clean-up. Foil packs work best on a two-inch bed of coals and will heat up quickly. You can use a few different types of foil packs. Remember that it is better to use too much foil than too little. Watch for steam and use potholders or oven mitts and long tongs to handle foil packs. Place them on baking sheets to move to and from your campfire.

CAMPFIRE SAFETY TIPS AND TRICKS

- Make sure it is legal to build a fire in your location.
- Use a fire pit, if available. Otherwise, build your fire on rock or dirt and construct a U-shaped perimeter with large rocks.
- Build your fire at least 8' away from flammable objects.
- Never use gas or kerosene on a fire as they pose a serious risk of explosion.
- Never leave a fire unattended.
- Don't build a fire if it's windy. Sparks can cause unintended fires.
- Protect hands with leather gloves or heavy oven mitts and use long tongs to prevent burns.
- Fill a bucket with water and keep it near the fire to douse flare-ups.
- Extinguish your fire by dousing it with plenty of water. Be sure all the coals, embers, and wood are wet and cool.
- If you don't have access to water, smother the fire with sand or dirt to extinguish it. You should still be sure all the coals, embers, and wood are completely cool.

Food wrapped in airtight foil packs will be steamed, not toasted or crunchy. For crisp foods, make and bake food in open foil pans. Make an open baking pan by using a double layer of heavy-duty foil molded over an upside-down pan of your choice. Leave extra length at all edges, fold them over, and crimp well for strength. You can also make a griddle for sautéing or frying foods over a campfire by covering a wire rack, grate, or grill with a double layer of heavy-duty foil. In this book, look for the foil symbol by a

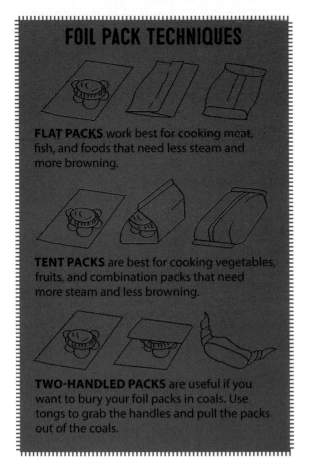

FOIL PACK TECHNIQUES

FLAT PACKS work best for cooking meat, fish, and foods that need less steam and more browning.

TENT PACKS are best for cooking vegetables, fruits, and combination packs that need more steam and less browning.

TWO-HANDLED PACKS are useful if you want to bury your foil packs in coals. Use tongs to grab the handles and pull the packs out of the coals.

recipe's name–this indicates that foil is the best cooking method.

Skewer Cooking

For authentic stick-cooked food:

- Choose long, sturdy, green twigs (not dry ones) so they won't break easily or catch on fire.
- Find those that are long enough to keep you away from the fire and sturdy enough to support the food.
- Whittle away the bark at the smallest end and sharpen to a point.

To use purchased sticks:

- Look for long roasting forks or sticks which come in a wide variety of shapes and sizes or regular metal skewers. Using short skewers will usually require a cooking surface such as a metal grate.

- Thick, heavy cooking sticks work well for heavy, sturdy foods; use thinner ones for light-weight, small, or delicate food.
- To keep food from spinning, use flat skewers, two side-by-side thin ones, or use a roasting fork with closely placed tines.

When assembling food on a stick, leave a little space between foods that require slow, even cooking (like dough or raw meat). If you don't want to hold food while you cook it, set a grate over the fire and lay the skewered food on top. A camping grate with legs or a grill grate work well. If you don't have a grate, use rocks to prop the food up over the fire!

Foil can be your best friend when campfire cooking. Use it to line your cooking grate for easy clean-up. Or wrap food in foil and pierce the foil with your cooking stick; hold over the fire to cook hobo-style. In this book, look for the stick symbol by a recipe's name–this indicates that a stick or skewer is the best cooking method.

Pie Iron Cooking

Make sure to preheat your pie iron before placing your sandwich on it. This will guarantee a crispy outside. If bread hangs outside the pie iron after closing it, use a sharp knife to trim off the excess. Or, try using larger slices of meats and vegetables, as opposed to small pieces. This will help prevent the fillings from tumbling out of the sandwich. There's nothing wrong with overstuffing your grilled cheese, but keep in mind the inner-most ingredients will take longer to get warm. It's also best to add sauces and spreads to the sandwich just before cooking so they don't have as much time to seep into the bread.

To cook, set the filled pie iron in hot coals, NOT IN FLAMES; flames will almost assure a burned exterior and a cold center.

Make sure you cover your pan to keep as much heat as possible around your sandwich. When the sandwich is nice and toasty, open the iron and slide the food onto your plate. Remember that pie irons stay hot! Don't touch anything but the handle, and do NOT set a pie iron on your lap or on a plastic plate or tablecloth. Food takes a bit longer to cook when the iron is cool; once it's hot

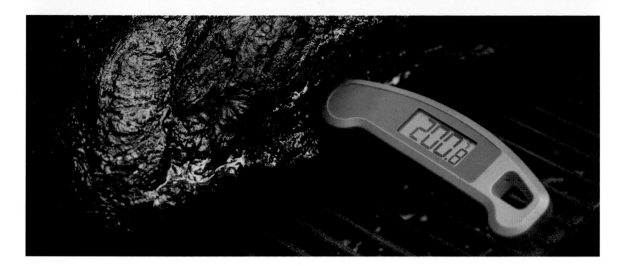

though, it cooks fast! Keep an eye on things by checking often. In this book, look for the pie iron symbol by a recipe's name–this indicates that a pie iron is the best cooking method.

COOKING TIMES WILL VARY

Speed of cooking depends on the temperature of the campfire and the type of food being cooked. Thick foods and frozen or refrigerated foods will take longer to cook than thinner foods or foods starting at room temperature.

You can adjust the temperature of your embers or coals by moving them apart and you can adjust the heat getting to your food by placing the food beside the coals on rocks or on a grill or grate above the coals. Turning your food often will also help evenly distribute the heat.

A Note on Campfire Cooking Temperatures

You can use the following method to judge the temperature of your campfire. Hold your hand about 4" over the coals. Count the number of seconds you can hold your hand in place before it gets too hot to keep it there.

- 2 seconds = about 500°F (High heat)
- 3 seconds = about 400°F (Medium-High heat)
- 4 seconds = about 350°F (Medium heat)
- 5 seconds = about 300°F (Low heat)

Food Temperature Safety

No matter the heat of your fire, always make sure your food is thoroughly cooked. Ground meat, chicken, and pork should be cooked until it is no longer pink and juices run clear. But color isn't a fool-proof guide. It is best to use a good meat thermometer to prevent under- or over-cooking. The USDA recommends the following minimum internal temperatures:

- Fish: 145°F
- Beef Roasts: 145°F (rare) to 160°F (medium) to 170°F (well-done)
- Ground Beef: 160°F
- Ground Poultry: 165°F
- Chicken Breasts: 170°F
- Pork (chops, tenderloins): 160°F
- Egg Dishes: 160°F
- Reheating Foods: 165°F or until hot and steaming

CAMPFIRE COOKING TEMPERATURES

How long can you hold your hand 4" over the coals?
- 2 seconds = about 500°F (High heat)
- 3 seconds = about 400°F (Medium-High heat)
- 4 seconds = about 350°F (Medium heat)
- 5 seconds = about 300°F (Low heat)

BREAKFAST

It's morning. The birds are chirping, the water in the lake is bubbling, and it's time to get that campfire crackling. Let's have some breakfast. From sweet to savory, we've got you covered.

CLASSIC BREAKFAST SANDWICH

Makes 1 sandwich per 2 bread slices  **PIE IRON**

INGREDIENTS

- 1 English muffin split or 2 white bread slices, one side buttered
- 1 egg, cooked over easy
- 4 leaves fresh baby spinach
- 1 slice sharp cheddar
- 2 slices bacon, crisp-cooked

Layer ingredients between bread slices and toast both sides.

THE LOX BAGEL

Makes 1 sandwich per 2 bread slices  **PIE IRON**

INGREDIENTS

- 1 everything bagel, split & one side buttered
- 1 tbsp. cream cheese, softened
- 1 slice gruyere cheese
- 2 oz. Nova lox
- 2 slices red onion
- 1 tsp. capers
- Fresh dill, to taste

Spread cream cheese on the unbuttered side of the bagel. Layer remaining ingredients between bagel halves and toast both sides.

FRENCH TOAST STACK SANDWICH

Makes 1 sandwich per 2 bread slices  PIE IRON

INGREDIENTS

Batter:
- 1 egg
- ¼ C.milk
- 1 tsp. vanilla
- ¼ tsp. cinnamon
- ¼ tsp. nutmeg

Sandwich:
- 2 thick-cut Italian bread slices
- 1 egg, scrambled
- 2 frozen hash browns, cooked
- 2 slices brie
- 2 bacon slices, crisp-cooked
- Salt, to taste

Combine ingredients for the batter. Dip one side of a bread slice in batter and place in the greased skillet. Layer remaining ingredients and top with another dipped bread slice. Toast both sides. Serve with maple syrup for dipping.

PEAR AND BACON BREAKFAST SANDWICH

Makes 1 sandwich per 2 bread slices  PIE IRON

INGREDIENTS

- 2 Multigrain bread slices, one side buttered
- 1 tbsp. fig jam
- 2 slices cheddar
- 3 strips bacon, crisp-cooked
- 1 pear, thinly sliced

Spread jam on the unbuttered side of the bread. Layer ingredients between slices and toast both sides.

THE BREAKFAST CLUB

Makes 1 sandwich per 2 bread slices  **PIE IRON**

INGREDIENTS

- 2 Multigrain bread slices, one side buttered
- 1 tbsp. raspberry jam
- 2 slices Provolone
- 2 thin slices Prosciutto
- 2 slices Deli roast turkey breast
- 1 egg, cooked over easy
- ½ cup fresh arugula
- Black pepper, to taste

Spread jam on the unbuttered side of the bread. Layer remaining ingredients between slices and toast both sides.

CHICKEN & WAFFLES SANDWICH

Makes 1 sandwich per 2 bread slices  **PIE IRON**

INGREDIENTS

- 2 frozen waffles, thawed & one side buttered
- 1 breaded chicken tender, cooked
- Hot sauce, to taste
- ½ cup shredded sharp cheddar
- Cajun seasoning, to taste
- ⅓ cup green onion, sliced

Layer ingredients between waffles and toast both sides. Serve with honey or maple syrup for dipping.

APPLE CINNAMON TOAST

Makes 1 sandwich per 2 bread slices  **PIE IRON**

INGREDIENTS

- 2 cinnamon raisin bread slices, one side buttered
- 1 green apple, crisped, cored, & thinly sliced
- 2 tbsps. mascarpone
- ¼ tsp. honey
- 2 tsps. brown sugar

Combine the mascarpone and honey and spread on the unbuttered side of the bread; add the apples and brown sugar. Sprinkle the outside of the sandwich with more brown sugar and toast both sides.

DONUT SANDWICH

Makes 1 sandwich per 2 bread slices **PIE IRON**

INGREDIENTS

- 1 maple-frosted donut, sliced in half & inside buttered
- 2 slices bacon, crisp-cooked
- 2 slices muenster

Layer ingredients between donut halves and toast both sides.

CAMPFIRE CINNAMON SPIRALS

Makes 8 servings **STICK**

Remove and separate rolls from a 12.4 oz. tube of refrigerated cinnamon rolls (8 ct.) and set aside enclosed frosting. Unroll each cinnamon roll and twist the dough around a cooking stick. Pinch together at the end so it clings to the stick during cooking. Heat slowly over warm embers, turning occasionally until the outside is golden brown and the inside is no longer doughy. Slide the rolls off the sticks and frost.

INGREDIENTS
- 12.4 oz. tube of refrigerated cinnamon rolls

COOKING TIP
Dough clings well to a wooden cooking stick, making it easier to cook.

CINNAMON PEACH FRENCH TOAST

Servings vary  **PIE IRON**

Whisk together the batter. Dip one side of the bread into the egg mixture and set into a greased pie iron, egg side down. Add cream cheese, pecans, and peaches. Top with another dipped bread slice, egg side up. Close the iron and toast both sides slowly over warm coals.

INGREDIENTS

Batter:

- 1 Egg
- ¼ cup milk
- 1 tsp. vanilla
- ¼ tsp. cinnamon
- ¼ tsp. sugar

Sandwich:

- 2 cinnamon swirl bread slices
- 1 oz. cream cheese
- 1 oz. chopped pecans
- 4 fresh peach slices

BELL PEPPER BASKET

Makes 4 servings **STICK**

Cut 2 bell peppers (any color) in half crosswise and scrape out all the seeds and membranes, leaving four shells. Push the ends of a long cooking fork carefully through each half so they hang like baskets. Crack an egg or two into each basket; hold over warm embers until egg is cooked. Season with salt, black pepper, and dill weed to taste.

For an omelet, whisk an egg with your favorite ingredients (try shredded cheese, ham, and veggies), then pour it into the pepper and cook as directed.

INGREDIENTS

- 2 bell peppers, any color
- 2-8 eggs
- Dill weed, to taste
- Salt, to taste
- Black pepper, to taste

COOKING TIP

To prevent scorching the pepper during cooking, cover the outside of the pepper half in foil. Then push the fork through both the foil and the pepper; add the egg, and cook as directed.

SUNRISE SAUSAGES

Makes 8 servings  **STICK**

Separate rolls from a 12.4 oz. tube of refrigerated cinnamon rolls (8 ct.) and unroll them, making ropes; set aside the frosting. Push both tines of a cooking fork through a precooked smoked sausage; wrap a cinnamon roll rope around it, pushing tightly to secure. Repeat with seven more sausages and the remaining ropes. Cook slowly over warm embers until the rolls are no longer doughy, turning to brown all sides, frost.

Sausage Dunkers: In a tall, narrow drinking glass, mix 1 C.. biscuit baking mix, 1 tbsp. sugar, ⅓ cup milk, and 1 egg until well blended. Cut a 14 oz. precooked smoked sausage ring into chunks and push a cooking stick through the length of each; dip into batter to coat. Cook above hot embers until golden brown. Serve with maple syrup.

INGREDIENTS

- 12.4 oz. tube of refrigerated cinnamon rolls
- 8 smoked sausages, precooked

For Sausage Dunkers:

- 14 oz. precooked smoked sausage ring
- 1 cup biscuit baking mix
- 1 egg
- Maple syrup

ALL-IN-ONE BREAKFAST KEBABS

Makes 4 servings  **STICK**

Ahead of time, parboil potatoes for just a few minutes, until slightly tender.

Cut oranges into wedges (don't peel), cut bell peppers into 1" pieces, and cut sausage links into chunks. On a stick, alternately skewer potatoes, oranges, bell peppers, whole kumquats, sausage, and pineapple. Brush marmalade liberally over the food.

Hold over hot embers until sausages are hot, fruit is lightly charred, and vegetables are crisp-tender, turning and brushing occasionally with marmalade. For good measure, brush a little more marmalade over everything just before serving.

Kumquats are probably the only citrus- type fruit you don't peel to eat – just pop them into your mouth! Their sweet- tart flavor mellows a bit when cooked over a fire.

INGREDIENTS

- 8 baby potatoes
- 2 oranges
- 2 green bell peppers
- 8 kumquats
- 6 brown-and-serve sausage links
- 1 cup pineapple chunks
- 1 cup orange marmalade, warmed

LUNCH

These lunch recipes will give you some lighter options, though still delicious, to give you energy for your day ahead—and giving you a taste of what's to come for dinner!

STUFFED JALAPEÑO SANDWICH

Makes 1 sandwich per 2 bread slices  **PIE IRON**

INGREDIENTS

- 2 Italian bread slices, one side buttered
- 2 jalapeños, sliced lengthwise, seeds & membranes removed
- 1 tbsp. cream cheese, softened
- 2 slices sharp cheddar
- 2 slices Monterey Jack
- 3 slices bacon, crisp-cooked
- ¼ cup fresh cilantro, chopped

Stuff jalapeños with cream cheese and bake in an oven for 25 minutes at 375°. Layer ingredients between bread slices and toast both sides on greased pie iron.

ULTIMATE GREEK SANDWICH

Makes 1 sandwich per 2 bread slices  **PIE IRON**

INGREDIENTS

- 2 sourdough bread slices, one side buttered
- 1 tbsp. original-flavored hummus
- 1 slice provolone
- ⅓ cup red onion, sliced
- 2 slices deli roast turkey
- ⅓ cup roasted red peppers, sliced
- ⅓ cup cucumber, sliced
- ⅓ cup Kalamata olives, sliced
- 3 oz. feta crumbles

Spread hummus on the unbuttered side of the bread. Layer remaining ingredients between slices and toast both sides. Use as much or as little of each ingredient as you like.

CLASSIC ITALIAN

Makes 1 sandwich per 2 bread slices  **PIE IRON**

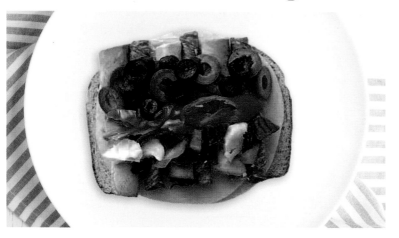

INGREDIENTS

- 2 sourdough bread slices, one side buttered
- 1 slice provolone
- 2 slices mozzarella
- 3 slices deli Genoa salami
- 3 slices deli ham
- ¼ cup Giardinela
- 2 tbsps. green and Kalamata olives
- 3 pepperoncini, sliced

Layer ingredients between bread slices and toast both sides on a greased skillet.

THE PEACHY-KEEN SANDWICH

Makes 1 sandwich per 2 bread slices  **PIE IRON**

INGREDIENTS

- 1 ciabatta roll, split & outsides buttered
- 1 tbsp. whole grain Dijon mustard
- 1 tbsp. peach preserves
- 2 Canadian bacon slices
- 1 peach, sliced
- ½ cup shredded fontina
- Fresh thyme, to taste

Spread mustard and preserves on the inside of the roll. Layer remaining ingredients between roll halves and toast both sides.

FRESH FROM THE GARDEN SANDWICH

Makes 1 sandwich per 2 bread slices  **PIE IRON**

INGREDIENTS

- 2 whole wheat bread slices, one side buttered
- 1 tbsp. cream cheese, softened
- 1 tsp. fresh chives, chopped
- ⅓ cup red onion, finely chopped
- 1 tomato, sliced
- 1 tsp. fresh basil, shredded
- Salt & pepper, to taste

Combine the cream cheese, chives, and onion and spread the mixture on the unbuttered side of the bread. Layer remaining ingredients between slices and toast both sides.

NACHO GRILLED CHEESE

Makes 1 sandwich per 2 bread slices  **PIE IRON**

INGREDIENTS

- 2 cheese bread slices, one side buttered
- 2 slices pepper jack
- ½ cup black beans, drained & rinsed
- ⅓ cup black olives, sliced
- ⅓ cup green onion, sliced
- 1 avocado, sliced
- 1 tbsp. salsa
- 4 nacho cheese tortilla chips

Layer ingredients between bread slices and toast both sides. Serve with sour cream for dipping.

APPLE GRUYERE SANDWICH

Makes 1 sandwich per 2 bread slices  **PIE IRON**

INGREDIENTS

- 2 multigrain bread slices, one side buttered
- 1 tbsp. mayo
- 1 crisp red apple, thinly sliced
- ½ cup shredded gruyere
- ¼ cup fresh arugula

Spread mayo on the unbuttered side of the bread. Layer remaining ingredients between slices and toast both sides.

FIELD OF GREENS SANDWICH

Makes 1 sandwich per 2 bread slices  **PIE IRON**

INGREDIENTS

- 2 multigrain bread slices, one side buttered
- 2 slices deli-roasted turkey
- ½ cup fresh arugula
- 1 avocado, sliced
- 1 tbsp. crumbled goat cheese

Layer ingredients between bread slices and toast both sides.

BROCCOLI CHEDDAR SANDWICH

Makes 1 sandwich per 2 bread slices  **PIE IRON**

INGREDIENTS

- 1 ciabatta roll, split & outsides buttered
- 2 slices sharp cheddar
- 1 tbsp. honey mustard
- 1 slice deli smoked turkey breast
- ½ cup broccoli, steamed
- Salt & pepper, to taste

Layer ingredients between roll halves and toast both sides on a greased skillet.

CRUNCHY SOURDOUGH SANDWICH

Makes 1 sandwich per 2 bread slices  **PIE IRON**

INGREDIENTS

- 2 sourdough bread slices, one side buttered
- 2 slices sharp cheddar
- 1 tomato, sliced
- 1 handful barbecue potato chips
- 2 pickled jalapeños
- 2 slices bacon, crisp-cooked

Layer ingredients between bread slices and toast both sides in a greased skillet.

CHEESY BRUSSELS SANDWICH

Makes 1 sandwich per 2 bread slices  **PIE IRON**

INGREDIENTS

- 2 whole grain bread slices, one side buttered
- ⅓ cup brussels sprouts, stems removed & thinly sliced
- 2 tsp. garlic, minced
- 1 tsp. balsamic vinegar
- 1 slice Havarti
- Salt & pepper, to taste

Sauté the Brussels sprouts and garlic; add salt, pepper, and balsamic vinegar. Layer all ingredients between bread.

EXTRA CHEESY GRILLED CHEESE

Makes 1 sandwich per 2 bread slices  **PIE IRON**

INGREDIENTS

- 2 Italian bread slices, one side buttered & sprinkled with shredded parmesan
- 2 slices provolone
- 2 slices fresh mozzarella
- ½ cup shredded Fontina
- ⅓ cup cheese curds

Layer ingredients between bread slices and toast both sides.

BERRY TURKEY SANDWICH

Makes 1 sandwich per 2 bread slices

INGREDIENTS

- 2 Italian bread slices, one side buttered
- 1 tbsp. red pepper jelly
- 2 slices deli smoked turkey breast
- 1 slice brie
- 2 medium strawberries, sliced
- 1 tsp. fresh basil

Spread the jelly on the unbuttered side of the bread. Layer the remaining ingredients between slices and toast both sides on a greased skillet.

HOT DOG SANDWICH

Makes 1 sandwich per 2 bread slices

INGREDIENTS

- 2 white bread slices, one side buttered
- 1 hot dog, sliced
- 1 slice Havarti
- 1 slice cheddar cheese
- 1 tbsp. pickle relish
- Ketchup and mustard, to taste
- ⅓ cup onion, sliced

Put all ingredients between unbuttered sides of bread. Toast to perfection.

LEFTOVER MEATLOAF SANDWICH

Makes 1 sandwich per 2 bread slices

INGREDIENTS

- 2 white bread slices, one side buttered
- 1 slice leftover meatloaf
- 1 dill pickle, sliced
- 1 tbsp. ketchup or chili sauce
- 1 slice Monterey Jack
- Salt and black pepper, to taste

Layer all ingredients evenly between unbuttered sides of bread. Toast it up and dig in!

VEGGIN'-OUT WASABI SANDWICH

Makes 1 sandwich per 2 bread slices

INGREDIENTS

- 2 wheat bread slices, one side buttered
- 2 tsps. garlic salt
- ½ cup cucumber, sliced
- ½ cup cauliflower, chopped
- ¼ cup purple cabbage, chopped
- ¼ cup red bell pepper, chopped
- 1 tbsp. Wasabi sauce (see page 105)

Sprinkle garlic salt on buttered side of bread; put remaining ingredients between unbuttered sides. Toast until golden brown.

SNACKS

From popcorn to sweet potatoes, sandwiches and kebabs are great for snacking too!

MINI GREEK SANDWICHES

Makes 2 sandwiches per 2 bread slices **STICK**

Spread hummus onto sourdough bread; cut into quarters. Top two of the quarters with 1 cucumber slice, deli-sliced roast turkey, roasted red pepper, and sliced provolone cheese. Add the other bread quarters, hummus side in, to create two sandwiches. Butter the outside of the bread and push the sandwiches onto cooking forks, making sure everything gets skewered in place. Hold over hot embers until the bread is toasted and the cheese begins to melt

INGREDIENTS

- 1 slice sourdough bread
- 2 tbsps. hummus
- 2 cucumber slices
- 2 slices deli roast turkey
- 2 slices red pepper, roasted
- 2 slices provolone cheese

PROSCIUTTO & MOZZARELLA

Makes 4 servings  **STICK**

Carefully push cherry tomatoes and mini marinated mozzarella balls onto flat cooking sticks, weaving strips of prosciutto in between; brush with Italian dressing. Hold over medium embers until the tomatoes have softened slightly, the prosciutto is starting to brown around the edges, and the mozzarella is just beginning to melt. A quick and easy snack to munch on at any time.

INGREDIENTS

- 12 cherry tomatoes
- 12 mini marinated mozzarella balls
- 6 slices prosciutto
- 1 cup Italian dressing

SWEET POTATO WEDGES - 3 WAYS

Makes 18 servings  **STICK**

Basic Potato Prep

Scrub 3 large sweet potatoes and parboil until crisp-tender; drain and set aside until cool enough to handle. Slice each potato into six thick wedges (leaving the skin on) and coat as directed for each recipe on the following page.

Slide coated sweet potatoes crosswise onto side-by-side cooking sticks and set on a greased grate over medium-hot embers. Cook until tender, turning as needed to brown both sides.

Serve with the dip or sauce indicated in each recipe.

CINNAMON SWEET POTATOES

- 3 tbsps. olive oil
- ¼ tsp. pumpkin pie spice
- ⅛ tsp. cinnamon
- ⅛ tsp. nutmeg

For Cinnamon Dip:
- 4 oz. cream cheese, softened
- 1 tsp. brown sugar
- 1 tsp. maple syrup
- ⅛ tsp. pumpkin pie spice
- ⅛ tsp. cinnamon

To coat prepped sweet potatoes, toss parboiled wedges in a mixture of olive oil, pumpkin pie spice, cinnamon, and nutmeg.

Cinnamon Dip: Mix softened cream cheese, brown sugar, maple syrup, pumpkin pie spice, and cinnamon until fully combined.

CURRIED SWEET POTATO DIPPERS

- 1½ tsps. curry powder
- ½ tsp. cayenne pepper
- Salt, to taste
- Black pepper, to taste

For Cilantro Yogurt Sauce:
- 1 cup plain Greek yogurt
- 3 tbsps. fresh cilantro, chopped
- 1 tbsp. fresh mint, chopped
- 1 lime
- 2 tsps. honey
- ¼ tsp. salt

To coat prepped sweet potatoes, toss parboiled wedges in a mixture of curry powder, cayenne pepper, salt, and black pepper.

Cilantro Yogurt Sauce: Mix plain Greek yogurt, chopped fresh cilantro, chopped fresh mint, lime juice and zest, honey, and salt until fully combined.

SWEET & SPICY WEDGES

- ¼ cup olive oil
- 2 tbsps. brown sugar
- 1 tbsp. smoked paprika
- 1 tbsp. sea salt
- 2 tsps. chili powder
- ½ tsp. cayenne pepper

For Creamy Maple Sauce:
- ½ cup sour cream
- ¼ cup mayonnaise
- 2 tbsps. maple syrup
- Salt, to taste
- Black pepper, to taste

To coat prepped sweet potatoes, toss parboiled wedges in a mixture of olive oil, brown sugar, smoked paprika, sea salt, chili powder, and cayenne pepper.

Creamy Maple Sauce: Mix sour cream, mayonnaise, maple syrup, salt, and black pepper until fully combined.

POPCORN POUCHES

Makes 2 servings STICK FOIL

Pour vegetable oil and popcorn kernels on an 18" square of heavy-duty foil. Bring the corners of foil together to make a pouch and seal the edges closed, leaving room for popcorn to pop and expand. Tie both ends of the pouch to a cooking stick with string. Hold the pouch over a cooking fire and shake until corn is popped. Cool slightly before opening. Add any additional toppings into the bag. Mix and enjoy!

INGREDIENTS

- 2 tbsps. popcorn kernels
- 1 tbsp. vegetable oil

Optional Additions:

- Melted butter and salt
- M&Ms and roasted peanuts or cashews
- ½ tsp. taco seasoning and a handful of shredded cheddar cheese
- ½ tsp. garlic salt, onion salt, sugar, or your favorite seasoning
- 1 square melted white almond bark

STUFFED DILLS

Makes 6 servings **STICK**

Cut regular whole dill pickles in half lengthwise and scoop out a little from the centers, leaving a boat shape, pat dry with paper towels. Mix softened cream cheese, cheddar cheese, and minced garlic until well combined. Divide the mixture among half the pickles and cover with the other half; cut bacon strips in half and wrap one piece snugly around each pickle to hold the halves together. Slide onto long cooking sticks, catching the ends of the bacon to secure.

Cook over hot embers, turning often, until bacon is done, and everything is hot.

INGREDIENTS

- 6 regular whole dill pickles
- 6 bacon strips
- 4 oz. cream cheese, softened
- ¾ cup cheddar cheese, finely shredded
- 1 tsp. minced garlic

MUSHROOM DELIGHTS

Makes 4–6 servings  **STICK**

INGREDIENTS

- ¼ cup olive oil
- ¼ cup lemon juice
- 1 tbsp. fresh parsley, finely chopped, or 1 tbsp. dried parsley
- 1 tsp. sugar
- 1 tsp. salt
- ¼ tsp. black pepper
- ¼ tsp. cayenne pepper
- 1 tsp. minced garlic
- 1 tbsp. balsamic vinegar
- 1 lb. whole white or baby Portobello mushrooms

Ahead of time, in a resealable plastic bag, mix the oil, lemon juice, parsley, sugar, salt, black pepper, cayenne pepper, garlic, and vinegar. Cut the mushrooms in half lengthwise through the stem and add to the bag; seal, turn to coat, and chill for 45 minutes.

Carefully slide the mushrooms onto thin cooking sticks and set on a greased grate over a cooking fire for several minutes on each side until hot, softened, and slightly browned. Just like the name says – delightful!

CHEESY BACON DOGS

Makes 4 servings  **STICK**

Slice 1 string cheese stick lengthwise into four pieces. Cut a slit in each of 4 hot dogs, from one end to the other, without cutting through the bottom. Place one cheese piece into the slit of each hot dog and roll the whole thing in brown sugar. Wrap a bacon strip around each one to hold in the cheese, secure with toothpicks. Push both tines of a cooking fork through each hot dog bundle. Cook very slowly over hot embers until bacon is cooked, turning to brown all sides. Remove toothpicks and enjoy.

Frank Kabobs: Cut hot dogs and whole dill pickles into equal-sized chunks; thread alternately onto a cooking stick and heat over the fire until browned to your liking. Slide the food onto a bun and top with any toppings of your choice

INGREDIENTS

- 4 hot dogs
- 4 bacon strips
- 1 string cheese stick
- Brown sugar, to taste

For Frank Kabob:
- 4 hot dogs
- 4 whole dill pickles
- 4 hot dog buns

BACON-BACON-BACON

Who doesn't love bacon? These snacks are all wrapped in bacon, for your pleasure!

BACON & ASPARAGUS

Makes 4 servings  **STICK**

Discard the hard ends from medium-size fresh asparagus spears and cut spears in half crosswise. Cut bacon strips in thirds and wrap one piece around two asparagus pieces; thread onto two side-by-side flat cooking sticks, catching the ends of the bacon to secure. Repeat. Spritz with cooking spray and sprinkle lightly with grated Parmesan cheese and black pepper.

Cook over medium embers, turning several times, until bacon is done.

INGREDIENTS

- 4 stalks asparagus
- 4 bacon strips
- Parmesan cheese, grated, to taste
- Black pepper, to taste

CHEESY BABY REDS

Makes 4 servings STICK

INGREDIENTS

- 16 tiny red potatoes
- ¼ cup olive oil
- 1 tsp. garlic salt
- 1 tsp. black pepper
- ½ lb. farmer's or Havarti cheese, cut into small squares
- Chopped fresh or dried chives, optional
- Sour cream, optional

Ahead of time, parboil the potatoes until just barely crisp-tender; set aside until cool enough to handle.

In a big resealable plastic bag, mix the oil, 1 teaspoon garlic salt, and 1 teaspoon pepper. Slice off a little from one side of each potato to create a flat top and add the potatoes to the bag; seal, toss to coat, and chill for 1 hour.

Thread the coated potatoes onto flat, sturdy cooking sticks with all the flat sides facing the same direction; set on a grate, flat sides down over very hot embers. Cook until nicely browned. Flip so flat tops face up and set a cheese square on each. Let the cheese melt, then sprinkle with chives and a little more garlic salt and pepper.

Serve with sour cream if you'd like.

WRAPPED CANTALOUPE

Servings vary STICK

Use a melon baller to scoop the fruit from a cantaloupe. Wrap one precooked bacon strip (or a partial strip, depending on size) around each cantaloupe ball and push onto flat cooking sticks (or two side-by-side ones), catching the ends of the bacon to secure.

Heat over hot embers, turning often, until bacon is crisp.

INGREDIENTS

- 1 cantaloupe
- 1 pack bacon strips, precooked

DINNER

Depending on what kind of day you've had, how many people are camping with you, or even what supplies you have handy, these dinner recipes are sure to please even the pickiest eater–or the barest cabinet.

COBB SANDWICH

Makes 1 sandwich per 2 bread slices  **PIE IRON**

INGREDIENTS

- 2 whole wheat bread slices, one side buttered
- 1 boneless, skinless chicken breast, cooked & sliced
- 2 slices bacon, crisp-cooked
- 1 avocado, sliced
- 1 egg, hard-cooked
- ½ cup shredded gouda
- ½ cup blue cheese crumbles

Layer ingredients between bread slices and toast both sides.

SPAGHETTI SANDWICH

Makes 1 sandwich per 2 bread slices  **PIE IRON**

INGREDIENTS

- 2 Italian bread slices, one side buttered & sprinkled with garlic salt
- 1 cup prepared spaghetti with sauce
- ½ cup shredded romano
- 2 tsp. Italian seasoning

Layer all ingredients between bread slices and toast both sides.

THE CORDON BLEU

Makes 1 sandwich per 2 bread slices  **PIE IRON**

INGREDIENTS

- 2 sourdough bread slices, one side buttered
- 1 tbsp. mayo
- 1 tbsp. dijon mustard
- 1 boneless, skinless chicken breast, cooked & sliced
- 2 slices prosciutto
- ½ cup shredded gruyere
- 1 tsp. fresh thyme

Combine the mayo and mustard. Layer all ingredients between bread slices and toast both sides.

TOASTED CHICKEN SANDWICH

Makes 1 sandwich per 2 bread slices  **PIE IRON**

INGREDIENTS

- 2 sourdough bread slices, one side buttered
- 1 boneless, skinless chicken breast, cooked & shredded
- 1 tbsp. barbecue sauce
- ⅓ cup red onion, sliced
- 2 slices provolone
- 2 tsps. fresh cilantro, chopped

Combine the shredded chicken and barbecue sauce. Layer all ingredients between bread slices and toast both sides.

BBQ CHICKEN SANDWICH

Makes 1 sandwich per 2 bread slices  **PIE IRON**

Set one slice of bread, butter side down, in a pie iron. Add cheddar and Gouda cheeses, chicken, onion, and BBQ sauce. Top with another bread slice, butter side up. Close the iron, trim as needed, and cook over hot coals, toasting both sides. Use unsmoked Gouda if you want the cheese meltier.

INGREDIENTS

- 2 white bread slices, one side buttered
- 1 slice cheddar
- 1 slice smoked Gouda
- 1 cup cooked chicken
- ⅓ cup red onion, sliced
- 2 tbsps. BBQ sauce

ROAST BEEF SANDWICH

Makes 1 sandwich per 2 bread slices  PIE IRON

INGREDIENTS

- 2 multigrain bread slices, one side buttered
- 2 tbsps. red onion, sliced
- 1 tbsp. balsamic vinegar
- Salt, to taste
- 1 tbsp. mayo
- 1 tbsp. prepared horseradish
- 5 leaves fresh baby spinach
- 2 slices deli roast beef
- 2 tsps. blue cheese crumbles

Sauté the onion; remove from heat and add the vinegar and salt. Combine the mayo and horseradish and spread on the unbuttered side of the bread. Layer all ingredients between slices and toast both sides.

CAPRESE SANDWICH

Makes 1 sandwich per 2 bread slices  PIE IRON

INGREDIENTS

- 2 Italian bread slices, one side buttered
- 1 boneless, skinless chicken breast
- 1 tsp. garlic powder
- 1 tsp. Italian seasoning
- Black pepper, to taste
- 3 slices fresh mozzarella
- 1 tomato, sliced
- 1 tbsp. fresh basil, chopped

Cook chicken in a skillet and season with garlic powder, Italian seasoning, and pepper. Layer all ingredients between bread slices and toast both sides. Serve with balsamic glaze for dipping.

CHICKEN POT PIE POCKET

Makes 1 serving  PIE IRON

Grease a pie iron and cut pie crust to fit. Line one side of the iron with crust. Add onion, chicken, veggies, salt, pepper, and a few spoonfuls of soup. Top with another pie crust, pressing edges together. Close the iron and cook slowly in warm coals, adding a few coals on top to speed things along if you're really hungry. When the crust is golden and flaky, it's done.

INGREDIENTS

- 1 refrigerated pie crust
- 1 onion
- 1 cup cooked chicken
- 1 canned mixed veggies, drained
- Salt and pepper, to taste
- 1 can cream of chicken soup

SHRIMP SANDWICH

Makes 1 sandwich per 2 bread slices  PIE IRON

INGREDIENTS

- 2 sourdough bread slices, one side buttered
- 2 tbsps. cream cheese, softened
- 1 tbsp. green onion, sliced
- 1 tsp. garlic salt
- 1 tbsp. soy sauce
- 2 tsps. worcestershire sauce
- Black pepper, to taste
- 1 cup cooked shrimp

Combine cream cheese, green onion, garlic salt, soy sauce, Worcestershire sauce, and black pepper and spread on the unbuttered side of the bread. Add the shrimp and toast both sides.

GOUDA MUSHROOM

Makes 1 sandwich per 2 bread slices  PIE IRON

INGREDIENTS

- 2 sourdough bread slices, one side buttered & sprinkled with garlic salt
- 2 portobello mushrooms, sliced
- 1 tsp. garlic, minced
- 2 tbsps. cream cheese, softened
- ⅓ cup fresh baby spinach
- ½ cup shredded gouda
- 1 tbsp. fresh chives, chopped
- Salt, to taste
- Black pepper, to taste

Sauté the mushrooms and garlic. Spread cream cheese on the unbuttered side of the bread. Layer all ingredients between slices and toast both sides.

TOASTED TURKEY SANDWICH

Makes 1 sandwich per 2 bread slices  PIE IRON

INGREDIENTS

- 2 sourdough bread slices, one side buttered
- 1 tbsp. port wine cheese spread
- 2 slices provolone
- 2 slices deli roast turkey breast
- 1 tomato, sliced
- 2 slices bacon, crisp-cooked
- Black pepper, to taste

Spread the port wine cheese on the unbuttered side of the bread. Layer remaining ingredients and toast both sides.

PROSCIUTTO AND BRIE SANDWICH

Makes 1 sandwich per 2 bread slices  PIE IRON

INGREDIENTS

- 2 sourdough bread slices, one side buttered
- 2 slices brie
- 2 slices prosciutto
- ⅓ cup fresh arugula

Layer ingredients between bread slices and toast both sides.

THE FRENCHMAN

Makes 1 sandwich per 2 bread slices  PIE IRON

INGREDIENTS

- 6" French bread loaf, split & one side buttered
- 2 slices gruyere
- 2 slices deli ham
- 2 sweet gherkins, sliced
- 1 tbsp. dijon mustard
- 2 tsps. dried tarragon
- Black pepper, to taste

Layer ingredients between bread halves and toast both sides.

THE OKTOBER-FEAST

Makes 1 sandwich per 2 bread slices  PIE IRON

INGREDIENTS

- Pretzel roll, split & outsides buttered
- 3 slices muenster
- 1 tbsp. honey mustard
- 1 brat, cooked & sliced in half lengthwise
- ½ cup coleslaw
- 1 tsp. caraway seed

Layer ingredients between roll halves and toast both sides.

CHICKEN BACON RANCH WRAP

Makes 1 wrap per 2 torillas  **PIE IRON**

Grease a pie iron and cut a tortilla to fit. Pile on some chicken and bacon, add both cheeses, and drizzle with dressing; season to taste. Top with another tortilla, cut to fit. Toast in hot coals until golden brown on the outside and hot and melty on the inside.

INGREDIENTS
- 2 flour tortillas
- ½ cup cooked chicken
- 3 slices cooked bacon
- ½ cup shredded mozzarella
- 1 tbsp. shredded parmesan
- 2 tbsps. ranch dressing
- 2 tsps. garlic powder
- Black pepper, to taste

MEAT & POTATOES SANDWICH

Makes 1 sandwich per 2 bread slices  PIE IRON

INGREDIENTS

- 2 French bread slices, one side buttered & sprinkled with garlic salt
- 5 oz. top sirloin steak
- ⅓ cup yellow onion, sliced
- 1 potato, thinly sliced
- Salt, to taste
- Black pepper, to taste
- 1 slice provolone
- ⅓ cup green onion, sliced

Cook and season the steak to your liking; thinly slice. Sauté onion and potato; season with salt & pepper. Layer all ingredients between bread slices and toast both sides.

GUACAMOLE GALORE

Makes 1 sandwich per 2 bread slices  PIE IRON

INGREDIENTS

- 2 sourdough bread slices, one side buttered
- 2 tbsps. guacamole
- 3 slices bacon, crisp-cooked
- ½ cup Colby Jack
- ⅓ cup tortilla chips, crumbled

Spread guacamole on the unbuttered side of the bread. Layer ingredients between bread slices and toast both sides.

STROMBOLI SANDWICH

Makes 1 sandwich per 2 bread slices  PIE IRON

INGREDIENTS

- 6" French bread loaf, split & one side buttered
- 2 tbsps. pizza sauce
- 1 cup shredded Mozzerella
- 5 slices deli Genoa salami
- 5 slices deli Capicola ham
- 1 red onion, sliced
- 3 pepperoncini, sliced
- 1 cup sun-dried tomatoes
- 1 tbsp. shredded Parmesan

Spread pizza sauce on the unbuttered side of the bread. Layer remaining ingredients between slices and toast both sides.

SLOPPY JOE

Makes 4 servings  PIE IRON

INGREDIENTS

- 8 sourdough bread slices, one side buttered
- 1 lb. ground turkey, chicken, beef, or pork
- 2 tbsps. barbecue sauce
- 3 slices American cheese
- 1 bag plain wavy potato chips
- 2 dill pickles, sliced

Cook the ground meat until browned. Add the barbecue sauce and let simmer. Layer all ingredients between bread slices and toast both sides.

PIE IRON BLT

Makes 1 sandwich per 2 bread slices  PIE IRON

Set one slice of bread, butter side down, in a pie iron. Spread with mayo and add some tomato and bacon. Top with another bread slice, butter side up. Close the iron, trim as needed, and cook over hot coals, toasting both sides. Slide sandwich out of pie iron and wrap in a lettuce leaf. Put lettuce inside sandwich if you'd like.

INGREDIENTS

- 2 Italian bread slices, buttered on one side
- 1 tbsp. mayo
- 1 tomato, sliced
- 2 slices cooked bacon
- Lettuce leaves for serving

CLASSIC REUBEN

Makes 1 sandwich per 2 bread slices  PIE IRON

INGREDIENTS

- 2 slices marble rye bread, one side buttered
- ½ cup sauerkraut, drained
- 3 slices deli corned beef
- ½ cup swiss cheese, shredded
- 1 tbsp. thousand Island dressing

Layer ingredients between bread slices and toast both sides.

CHIPOTLE MUSHROOM SANDWICH

Makes 1 sandwich per 2 bread slices  PIE IRON

INGREDIENTS

- 6" French bread loaf, split & one side buttered
- 2 Baby Bella mushrooms, sliced
- 1 tbsp. cream cheese, softened
- 1½ cups chipotle peppers in adobo sauce, sliced
- ½ cup shredded cheddar
- 2 tsps. fresh cilantro, chopped

Sauté mushrooms. Spread the cream cheese on the unbuttered side of the bread. Layer all ingredients between halves and toast both sides.

MAC AND CHEESE SAMMY

Makes 1 sandwich per 2 bread slices  PIE IRON

INGREDIENTS

- Italian bread slices, one side buttered & sprinkled with garlic powder
- 1 cup prepared macaroni & cheese
- 2 slices pancetta, pan-fried
- ½ cup shredded asiago

Layer ingredients between bread slices and toast both sides.

EASY PIZZA MUFFIN

Makes 1 sandwich, per 2 bread slices  PIE IRON

INGREDIENTS

- 1 English muffin, halved crosswise
- 1 tbsp. pizza sauce
- 2 tsps. Italian seasoning
- 2 slices pepperoni
- ½ cup cooked sausage
- 1 bell pepper, sliced
- ⅓ cup red onion, sliced
- ⅓ c. black olives
- ⅓ cup mushrooms, sliced
- ½ cup Cheddar and mozzarella cheeses

Grease a pie iron and set an English muffin half in one side. Add remaining ingredients or use any of your favorite toppings. Top with another English muffin half. Close the iron and cook over hot coals to toast both sides. Serve with more pizza sauce.

LUAU SANDWICH

Makes 1 sandwich per 2 bread slices  PIE IRON

Spread the pizza sauce on the unbuttered side of the bread. Layer remaining ingredients between slices and toast both sides.

INGREDIENTS

- 2 Texas toast slices, one side buttered
- 2 tbsps. pizza sauce
- 2 slices deli ham
- 2 pineapple rings
- ½ cup shredded mozzarella
- 3 pickled jalapeños

THE BUFFALO RANCH

Makes 1 sandwich per 2 bread slices  **PIE IRON**

INGREDIENTS

- 2 sourdough bread slices, one side buttered
- 2 tbsps. buffalo sauce
- 1 slice provolone
- 2 breaded chicken tenders, cooked
- 1 tbsp. ranch dressing
- ⅓ cup Blue cheese crumbles
- ⅓ cup fresh chives, chopped

Layer ingredients between bread slices and toast both sides.

TURKEY PESTO SANDWICH

Makes 1 sandwich per 2 bread slices **PIE IRON**

INGREDIENTS

- 6" French bread loaf, split, one side buttered
- ½ cup basil pesto
- 4 slices mozzarella
- 1 avocado, sliced
- 5 slices deli roast turkey
- 1 tomato, sliced
- Black pepper, to taste

Layer ingredients between bread slices and toast both sides.

DILL CORNED BEEF SANDWICH

Makes 1 sandwich per 2 bread slices  PIE IRON

INGREDIENTS

- 2 sourdough bread slices, one side buttered
- 1 tbsp. sour cream
- 1 tbsp. mayo
- 2 slices deli corned beef
- ⅓ cup dill pickle relish
- ½ cup dill-flavored Monterey Jack cheese
- ⅓ cup green onion, finely chopped

Mix equal amounts of sour cream and mayo and spread on the unbuttered side of the bread. Layer remaining ingredients and toast both sides.

SPINACH ARTICHOKE SANDWICH

Makes 1 sandwich per 2 bread slices  PIE IRON

INGREDIENTS

- 2 sourdough bread slices, one side buttered
- 1 tbsp. frozen chopped spinach
- 1 tbsp. canned artichoke hearts
- 1 tbsp. mayo
- 1 tsp. garlic powder
- Salt, to taste
- Black pepper, to taste
- ½ cup shredded mozzarella
- 1 tbsp. shredded parmesan

Thaw and squeeze excess moisture from the spinach and drain and chop the artichokes. Mix equal parts spinach, artichokes, and mayo; season with garlic powder, salt, and pepper and spread on unbuttered side of bread. Add cheeses and toast both sides.

CHICKEN PARM SANDWICH

Makes 1 sandwich per 2 bread slices **PIE IRON**

INGREDIENTS

- 2 sourdough bread slices, one side buttered
- 2 tbsps. marinara sauce
- 2 breaded chicken tenders, cooked & sliced
- ½ cup shredded mozzarella
- 1 tbsp. shredded parmesan
- 1 tsp. fresh basil
- Black pepper, to taste

Spread marinara sauce on the unbuttered side of the bread. Layer remaining ingredients between slices and toast both sides.

CHIPOTLE & HERB SANDWICH

Makes 1 sandwich per 2 bread slices  **PIE IRON**

INGREDIENTS

- Pretzel roll, split & outsides buttered
- 1 tbsp. mayo
- 2 tsps. lime juice
- 2 tsps. chipotle chili powder
- Salt, to taste
- Black pepper, to taste
- 1 slice garlic & herb flavored Boursin
- 1 slice deli roast beef
- ⅓ cup red onion, sliced
- ⅓ cup radishes, thinly sliced
- 1 tsp. dried rosemary

Mix mayo, lime juice, chili powder, salt, and pepper; spread on the unbuttered side of the roll. Layer remaining ingredients between roll halves and toast both sides.

MEATBALL SUBS

Makes 4–6 servings STICK

INGREDIENTS

- 1½ lbs. ground beef
- 1 cup panko breadcrumbs
- 4 eggs
- ½ cup milk
- ¾ cup grated Parmesan or Romano cheese, plus more for sprinkling
- 1 tsp. onion salt
- 1 tsp. minced garlic
- 1 tbsp. dried parsley
- 1 tbsp. dried basil
- 1 onion, cut into chunks
- 4 to 6 sub buns
- 1 cup spaghetti sauce, warmed, optional

Ahead of time, mix ground beef, breadcrumbs, eggs, milk, cheese, onion salt, garlic, parsley, and basil until well combined. Roll the mixture into 1½" balls and chill for several hours. Keep meatballs chilled until ready to cook.

Thread several chilled meatballs onto a cooking stick (leaving a little space in between so they cook evenly) and thread the onion chunks onto a separate stick. Cook over hot embers until meatballs are done and onions are crisp-tender and lightly charred, turning occasionally to brown all sides.

Serve meatballs and onions on buns with warm spaghetti sauce and a sprinkling of cheese.

THE HOT POTATO

Makes 1 sandwich per 2 bread slices  PIE IRON

INGREDIENTS

- 2 Texas toast slices, one side buttered
- 1 potato, sliced
- Salt, to taste
- Black pepper, to taste
- 1 tsp. garlic powder
- 1 tbsp. sour cream
- ½ cup shredded cheddar
- 2 slices bacon, crisp-cooked
- 1 tbsp. fresh chives, chopped

Fry potato slices; season with salt, pepper, and garlic powder. Spread sour cream on the unbuttered side of the bread. Layer all ingredients between slices and toast both sides.

FAJITA SANDWICH

Makes 1 sandwich per 2 bread slices  PIE IRON

INGREDIENTS

- 2 potato bread slices, one side buttered
- ¼ cup red onion, sliced
- ¼ cup bell pepper, sliced
- ¼ cup zucchini, thinly sliced
- 1 tbsp. fajita seasoning
- 1 queso fresco chipotle cheese wedge
- 1 tbsp. chimichurri sauce
- 1 slice pepper jack

Sauté veggies; stir in seasoning. Spread cheese wedge and chimichurri on unbuttered side of bread. Layer all ingredients between slices and toast both sides.

TROPICAL TURKEY TZATZIKI

Makes 6–8 servings  **STICK**

Ahead of time, in a big resealable plastic bag, combine the coconut milk, garlic, brown sugar, turmeric, salt, cumin, ginger, coriander, and cilantro or chives; turn to mix. Cut the turkey into strips, ¼" to ½" thick and about 1" wide and add them to the bag. Seal the bag and chill for 2 hours.

Weave the turkey strips onto cooking sticks alternating lemon and lime slices between the loops and set on a greased grate over medium embers until cooked through, turning to brown both sides.

Serve with Tzatziki Sauce.

Tzatziki Sauce: Stir together 2 (5.3 oz.) containers (about ⅓ C.) plain Greek yogurt, 1 small cucumber (diced & patted dry), the juice of 1 lemon, 2 tbsps. chopped fresh dill, 1 tbsp. minced garlic, and salt and black pepper to taste.

INGREDIENTS

- 1 cup coconut milk
- 1 tbsp. minced garlic
- 1 tbsp. brown sugar
- 2 tsps. ground turmeric
- 1½ tsps. salt
- 1 tsp. ground cumin
- ½ tsp. ground ginger
- ½ tsp. ground coriander
- ¼ cup chopped fresh cilantro or chives
- 1½ to 2 lbs. turkey tenderloin
- Lemon and lime slices
- Tzatziki Sauce (recipe included)

MUSHROOM & SPINACH ALFREDO CALZONE

Makes 1 serving ● PIE IRON

Grease a pie iron. Roll dough thin and cut to fit iron; press one piece inside. Add remaining ingredients and top with another dough piece. Close the iron and cook slowly over warm coals to assure the dough cooks completely, turning to toast both sides.

INGREDIENTS

- Refrigerated pizza dough
- 1 cup frozen spinach, thawed & drained
- 1 onion, sliced
- 1 bell pepper, sliced
- 2 mushrooms, sliced
- 1 tsp. minced garlic
- 1 cup alfredo sauce
- 1 cup shredded provolone
- Salt, to taste
- Black pepper, to taste

CUBAN SANDWICH

Makes 1 sandwich per 2 bread slices  **PIE IRON**

INGREDIENTS

- 2 sourdough bread slices, one side buttered
- 2 slices swiss cheese
- ½ cup shredded cooked pork roast
- 2 Canadian bacon slice
- 1 dill pickle, sliced
- 1 tbsp. yellow mustard

Layer ingredients between bread slices and toast both sides.

CHILI CAMPWICH

Makes 1 sandwich per 2 bread slices  **PIE IRON**

INGREDIENTS

- 2 Texas Toast slices, one side buttered
- 1 cup prepared chili
- ⅓ cup corn chips
- 1 slice cheddar
- ⅓ cup red onion, chopped

Drain excess liquid from chili. Pile everything between unbuttered sides of bread slices then toast. Arrange evenly.

SPICY SAUSAGE SANDWICH

Makes 1 sandwich per 2 bread slices  PIE IRON

Butter one side of the bread slices; set one slice, butter side down, in a pie iron. Layer Gouda, chipotle cheddar, and Muenster cheeses, bell pepper, onion, and sausage on the bread. Now top with another bread slice, butter side up. Close, trim as needed, and toast both sides.

INGREDIENTS

- 2 rye bread slices, buttered on one side
- 1 slice gouda
- 1 slice Chipotle cheddar
- 1 slice Muenster
- ⅓ cup green bell pepper, sliced
- ⅓ cup onion, sliced
- 1 cooked Italian sausage, sliced

NOT-SO-SLOPPY JOE

Servings vary  PIE IRON

INGREDIENTS

- 1 English muffin, halved crosswise
- 1 lb. ground pork or beef
- 1 (15 oz.) can sloppy joe sauce
- 1 red bell pepper
- 1 dill pickle, sliced
- 1 green onion, chopped
- Yellow mustard

Prepare sloppy joe mixture with ground meat according to sauce instructions. Put all ingredients between English muffin halves and toast in a greased pie iron.

TURKEY & CRANBERRY SANDWICH

Makes 1 sandwich per 2 bread slices  PIE IRON

INGREDIENTS

- 2 sourdough bread slices, one side buttered
- ½ cup cooked turkey
- ½ cup jellied cranberry sauce
- 1 slice Havarti
- ½ cup spreadable brie
- 1 tsp. dried sage or seasonings of choice

Layer ingredients between bread slices, buttered sides out; toast and pretend it's Thanksgiving.

CHICKEN CHIMICHANGA

Servings vary  **PIE IRON**

Grease a pie iron and cut a tortilla to fit. Layer on rice, cheese, and chicken; season to taste and top with another tortilla, cut to fit. Close, trim as needed, and toast both sides. Remove from iron and add toppings.

Alternate method: Put ingredients into the center of a whole tortilla; fold in all sides to enclose filling, set seam side down in pie iron, and toast.

INGREDIENTS

- 1-2 flour tortillas
- 1-2 cup prepared Spanish rice
- 1 cup shredded cheddar
- 1 cup cooked chicken
- 2 tsps. ground cumin
- 2 tsps. garlic salt
- 1 tsp. cayenne pepper
- Your favorite toppings for serving

ISLAND WRAP

Makes 1 wrap per 2 tortillas  **PIE IRON**

INGREDIENTS

- 2 flour tortillas
- ½ cup Monterey Jack
- ½ cup cooked ham
- 2 slices cooked bacon
- ½ cup crushed pineapple, drained
- 2 tbsps. BBQ sauce
- ⅓ cup pickled banana peppers

Cut tortillas a little bigger than a pie iron; grease the iron and press one tortilla inside. Top tortilla with cheese, ham, bacon, pineapple, BBQ sauce, and banana peppers. Add another tortilla piece. Close, trim as needed, and toast both sides. Serve with more BBQ sauce for dipping.

CAMPIN' SEAFOOD DINNER

Makes 4 servings STICK

Ahead of time, in a big resealable plastic bag, combine vegetable oil, lemon juice, soy sauce, minced garlic, ground ginger, onion powder, and black pepper; seal the bag and shake to combine. Add sea scallops (cut in half if large); seal, toss to coat, and chill for several hours. Discard marinade and thread scallops onto cooking sticks along with fresh pineapple and zucchini chunks. Cook over medium-hot embers until scallops are done, basting frequently with soy sauce and/or lemon juice.

INGREDIENTS

- 2 tbsps. vegetable oil
- 1 tbsp. lemon juice
- 1 tbsp. soy sauce
- ½ tsp. minced garlic
- ¾ tsp. ground ginger
- ¼ tsp. onion powder
- ½ tsp. black pepper
- 1 lb. sea scallops
- 1 zucchini, ½ inch slices
- Fresh pineapple chunks

CAMPIN' SEAFOOD DINNER

Makes 4 servings **STICK**

Ahead of time, in a big resealable plastic bag, combine vegetable oil, lemon juice, soy sauce, minced garlic, ground ginger, onion powder, and black pepper; seal the bag and shake to combine. Add sea scallops (cut in half if large); seal, toss to coat, and chill for several hours. Discard marinade and thread scallops onto cooking sticks along with fresh pineapple and zucchini chunks. Cook over medium-hot embers until scallops are done, basting frequently with soy sauce and/or lemon juice.

INGREDIENTS

- 2 tbsps. vegetable oil
- 1 tbsp. lemon juice
- 1 tbsp. soy sauce
- ½ tsp. minced garlic
- ¾ tsp. ground ginger
- ¼ tsp. onion powder
- ½ tsp. black pepper
- 1 lb. sea scallops
- 1 zucchini, ½ inch slices
- Fresh pineapple chunks

JAMAICAN JERK & MELON

Makes 6 servings **STICK**

Ahead of time, mix vegetable oil and Jamaican jerk seasoning in a big resealable plastic bag. Cut boneless, skinless chicken breasts into ½ x 1½" chunks and cut a yellow onion and pablano peppers into 1½ to 2" chunks; add everything to the bag, seal, and turn to coat. Chill at least 30 minutes. Cut cantaloupe and honeydew melon into 1½ to 2" chunks and alternately skewer onto cooking sticks with the chicken (pieces folded in half), the onion, and the peppers. Hold over medium-hot embers until cooked through, turning to brown evenly.

Toward the end of cooking, brush with a mixture of honey and vegetable oil. Drizzle on a little honey and sprinkle with more jerk seasoning before serving if you'd like.

INGREDIENTS

- 2 tbsps. vegetable oil
- 4 tsp. Jamaican jerk seasoning
- 1½ lbs. boneless, skinless chicken breasts
- 1 yellow onion
- 3 or 4 poblano peppers
- Cantaloupe
- Honeydew melon
- 1½ tsps. honey
- 1½ tsps. vegetable oil

LOADED PIZZA STICKS

Makes 6 servings **STICK**

INGREDIENTS

- 1 (13.8 oz.) tube refrigerated pizza crust dough
- Flour, optional
- Olive oil
- Italian seasoning
- Grated Parmesan or Romano cheese
- 1 (19 oz.) pkg. cooked Italian sausage links, cut into chunks
- Small whole mushrooms
- Cherry tomatoes
- 1 or 2 onions, cut into chunks
- 1 or 2 green bell peppers, cut into chunks
- 1 (3.5 oz.) pkg. pepperoni slices
- Pizza sauce, warmed, optional

Press out the pizza dough on a floured or oiled surface to make a 9 x 12" rectangle; brush with olive oil and sprinkle with Italian seasoning and cheese. Cut crosswise into 12 strips, 1" wide.

Push one end of a dough strip onto a long cooking stick, then alternately thread on sausage, mushrooms, tomatoes, onions, bell peppers, and several pepperoni slices, threading the dough strip back onto the stick several times in between to secure. Wrap the end of the dough strip around and over the tip of the stick one last time, pinching well to seal. Repeat with the remaining ingredients.

Hold over medium embers, rotating slowly until golden brown all around and the dough is cooked through.

Serve with warmed pizza sauce if you'd like.

COOKING TIP

Whenever you're cooking dough over the fire, the trick is to cook slowly. Cook too fast and the dough won't be done in the middle, and that makes for unhappy campers. Patience just takes a little practice.

SAVORY STEAK & VEGGIES KEBAB

Makes 6 servings  STICK

Ahead of time, stir together the lemon juice, oil, Worcestershire sauce, paprika, garlic, sugar, salt, and pepper sauce; pour ½ cup of the mixture into a big resealable plastic bag and pour the remainder into a separate small container.

Cut the steak into 1" cubes and add them to the bag with the marinade; seal and turn bag to coat. Chill for at least 2 hours but no longer than overnight.

Cut onions and bell peppers into chunks. Discard the marinade from the bag and alternately thread beef, onion, bell peppers, and mushrooms onto a cooking stick.

Hold over hot embers until the steak reaches desired doneness, turning and basting frequently with the reserved marinade.

INGREDIENTS

- ⅔ cup lemon juice
- ¼ cup vegetable oil
- 4 tsp. Worcestershire sauce
- 2 tsps. paprika
- 2 tsps. minced garlic
- 1 tsp. sugar
- 1 tsp. salt
- ¼ tsp. hot pepper sauce
- 1½ lbs. beef sirloin steak
- 2 onions
- 2 green bell peppers
- ½ to 1 lb. fresh whole mushrooms

COOKING TIP

You want to cook over a fire? Bring plenty of matches and keep them dry by storing them in plastic containers rather than in matchboxes. There's nothing worse than rubbing sticks together forever trying to get your fire going.

CAJUN SHRIMP & SAUSAGE

Makes 6–8 servings **STICK**

Ahead of time, whisk together mayonnaise, lemon juice, and 1 tbsp. Cajun seasoning; chill until needed (up to 2 days). Mix olive oil and 1 tbsp. Cajun seasoning in a big resealable plastic bag. Using paper towels, pat dry raw shrimp and add to the bag; seal the bag and turn to coat. Slice fully cooked Cajun-style sausage into rounds the same thickness as the shrimp. Alternately thread shrimp and sausage onto cooking sticks and hold over medium-hot embers until cooked and hot. Serve with the chilled dipping sauce.

INGREDIENTS

- ½ cup mayonnaise
- 1 tbsp. lemon juice
- 2 tbsps. Cajun seasoning
- 2 tsps. olive oil
- 1 lb. raw shrimp (40 to 50 ct., peeled and deveined)
- 1 (12 oz.) pkg. fully cooked Cajun-style sausage

CHINESE PORK RIBBONS

Makes 4 servings **STICK**

Ahead of time, in a big resealable plastic bag, mix the soy sauce, vinegar, oil, honey, 5-spice blend, pepper flakes, and garlic salt. Remove excess fat from the tenderloin and cut the meat into 12 strips, ¼" thick and about 5" long. Add the strips to the bag; seal and turn to coat. Chill for at least 4 hours but no more than 24 hours. Discard the marinade and thread pork strips accordion-style onto cooking sticks. Set sticks on an oiled grate over medium-hot embers and cook until the meat is done. Serve with peanut sauce.

DIY Chinese 5-Spice Blend: To make just enough for this recipe, mix 1 tsp. cinnamon, 1 tsp. crushed anise seed, ¼ tsp. crushed fennel seed, ¼ tsp. black pepper, and ⅛ tsp. ground cloves.

INGREDIENTS

- 3 tbsps. soy sauce
- 2 tbsps. rice wine vinegar
- 2 tbsps. olive oil
- 1 tsp. honey
- 2 to 3 tsp. Chinese 5-spice blend (recipe included)
- ½ to 1 tsp. red pepper flakes
- 1 tsp. garlic salt
- 1 lb. pork tenderloin
- Bottled peanut sauce

HOT DOG AND VEGGIE KEBAB

Makes 4–6 servings **STICK**

INGREDIENTS

- ⅓ cup white wine vinegar
- ⅓ cup olive oil
- 1 tsp. dried lemon peel
- ½ tsp. salt
- ½ tsp. black pepper
- ½ tsp. celery seed
- 1 medium zucchini
- 1 small eggplant
- ½ lb. whole mushrooms
- 4–6 hot dogs, cut into chunks

Ahead of time, in a big resealable plastic bag, mix the vinegar, oil, dried lemon peel, salt, pepper, and celery seed. Cut zucchini and eggplant into long ribbons, about ¼" thick; cut eggplant ribbons in half lengthwise if necessary so they're about the same width as the zucchini ribbons. Add the ribbons to the bag along with the mushrooms and hot dogs; seal the bag and turn to coat. Chill for at least 2 hours.

Discard the marinade and weave strips of vegetables onto cooking sticks, alternating the mushrooms and hot dog pieces between the loops. Cook over medium embers until vegetables are crisp-tender, turning often.

SESAME-GINGER BRAT K'BOBS

Makes 4–6 servings  STICK

INGREDIENTS

- ¾ cup purchased sesame-ginger marinade
- ¼ cup lime juice
- 2 bell peppers, any color
- 1 red onion
- 1 zucchini and/or yellow squash
- 1 (14 oz.) pkg. fully cooked brats
- Small whole white mushrooms

Ahead of time, pour the marinade and lime juice into a big resealable plastic bag. Cut the bell peppers, onion, squash, and brats into chunks and add them to the bag along with the mushrooms; seal the bag, turn to coat, and chill for 30 minutes.

Alternately thread the marinated food onto cooking sticks. Hold over a cooking fire until heated through, turning and brushing with the marinade occasionally.

COOKING TIP

The joy of cooking kabobs is the opportunity for nearly endless customization. Choose foods with similar cooking times or simply thread each type of food onto its own stick and cook separately; that way, if one item gets done quicker than the rest, you're not stuck with overcooked food.

FISH 'N' FOIL

Makes 4 servings STICK FOIL

Ahead of time, in a big resealable plastic bag, mix ⅓ c. olive oil, ¼ c. lemon juice, 1 tsp. dried basil, ½ tsp. dried thyme, ¼ tsp. salt, ¼ tsp. black pepper, and 1 tsp. garlic powder; add 1 lb. thawed cod fillets. Seal the bag, turn to coat, and set aside for 30 minutes. Line four 12 x 24" pieces of heavy-duty foil with parchment paper; spritz with cooking spray. Peel 1 spaghetti squash, remove seeds, and cut into ¼"-thick crosswise slices; lay a few slices on each lined foil piece. Add fresh green beans to each, drizzle with olive oil, sprinkle with salt and garlic powder, and top with some fish. Close parchment/foil around the food, sealing with tight, heavy folds; push the ends of a cooking fork through each pack, right below the folds. Hold over hot embers until cooked and tender.

INGREDIENTS

- Olive oil
- ¼ cup lemon juice
- 1 tsp. dried basil
- ½ tsp. dried thyme
- ¼ tsp. salt
- ¼ tsp. black pepper
- 1 tsp. garlic powder
- 1 lb. thawed cod fillets
- 1 spaghetti squash
- Fresh green beans

BALSAMIC STEAK KEBABS

Makes 6 servings **STICK**

INGREDIENTS

- 2 tsps. butter
- 2 tbsps. finely chopped shallot
- ¼ cup balsamic vinegar
- 2 tbsps. brown sugar
- ¼ cup beef broth
- 2 carrots
- 1 zucchini
- 1 red bell pepper
- ½ lb. asparagus, trimmed
- 1½ lbs. sirloin steak
- Worcestershire sauce
- Salt and black pepper to taste
- Mesquite steak seasoning

Ahead of time, melt the butter in a small pan and add the shallot; cook until softened. Stir in the vinegar, brown sugar, and broth. Bring to a boil, boiling until liquid is reduced to about half. Meanwhile, cut the carrots, zucchini, and bell pepper into matchsticks; toss into boiling water along with the asparagus and parboil for a few minutes, then drain. Cut the steak into eight equal pieces and pound ⅛" to ¼" thick; drizzle with a little Worcestershire sauce and let stand for 10 minutes. Top each steak piece with some of the parboiled vegetables and season with salt and pepper. One at a time, roll the steak around the vegetables and thread onto side-by-side cooking sticks, catching the ends of the steak to secure; repeat until all the bundles are skewered. Set aside 2 tablespoons of the balsamic mixture and brush the remainder over the bundles. Sprinkle with steak seasoning. Cook the sticks on an oiled grate over hot embers, until steak is cooked to your liking, turning to brown both sides. Brush with set-aside balsamic mixture before serving.

COOKING TIP

Precooked rice that you can purchase in a bag at the grocery store is a great staple to take along on camping trips. Simply heat it up over the fire (or use a microwave if you have one).

BUFFALO BISCUIT CUPS

Makes 8 servings  STICK · FOIL

On the end of a long, thick stick or wooden dowel, create a "cup" 3" to 4" in diameter by wrapping with layers of foil; cover with a longer piece of foil, wrapping and twisting it down and around the dowel to hold it in place. Spritz the cup lightly with cooking spray. (Having more than one of these is ideal!)

Separate biscuits; one at a time, lay them on a flat surface and press into a thin circle (without tearing them). Lay the biscuit over the end of the foil cup and press gently. Keep remaining biscuits chilled until needed.

Hold the biscuit above warm embers until nicely browned on the outside and no longer doughy in the middle, rotating often. Repeat with remaining biscuits. (If you're having trouble getting the cups done in the middle, remove from the dowel once browned and set on a rack, open side down, above hot embers; it'll only take a few minutes.)

Meanwhile, stir together the chicken, carrots, celery, onion, buffalo sauce, lemon juice, salt, pepper, and garlic powder.

Spritz a big piece of foil with cooking spray and dump half the chicken mixture in the center; bring the edges of the foil up around the filling and crimp several times to seal, making a thick, heavy fold. Repeat with more foil and the remaining chicken mixture. Push a cooking stick through the foil below the fold of each pack; hold over the heat until the filling is warm.

Divide the mixture among the biscuit cups and top with tomatoes, cheese, and dressing.

INGREDIENTS

- 1 (16.3 oz.) tube refrigerated biscuits (8 ct.)
- 2 lbs. boneless, skinless chicken thighs, cooked & shredded
- ½ cup finely chopped carrots
- ½ cup finely chopped celery
- ½ cup finely chopped red onion
- 4 to 5 tbsps. buffalo sauce
- 1 tsp. lemon juice
- Salt, black pepper, and garlic powder to taste
- Chopped tomatoes
- Shredded cheddar cheese
- Blue cheese dressing

COOKING TIP

These biscuit cups can be filled with just about anything. Try tuna salad, scrambled eggs, taco filling—even green bean casserole! Be creative and enjoy!

PORK & APPLE STICKS

Makes 4 servings STICK

INGREDIENTS

- 1 lb. pork tenderloin
- Salt, to taste
- 1 green bell pepper
- 1 onion
- 2 Gala apples
- Lemon juice
- 2 tsps. melted butter
- ½ cup applesauce
- ¼ cup finely chopped walnuts
- 2 tbsps. brown sugar

Remove excess fat from the tenderloin and cut the meat into 1" cubes; season with salt. Cut the bell pepper, onion, and apples into chunks; dip apples in lemon juice. Alternately thread the meat, vegetables, and fruit onto cooking sticks. Stir together the butter, applesauce, walnuts, and brown sugar and brush liberally over the food. Set on an oiled grate and cook over hot embers until the pork is done, turning to brown both sides.

FIRESIDE SALMON TACOS

Makes 4 servings  **STICK**

INGREDIENTS

- 1 tbsp. paprika
- 1 tsp. cayenne pepper
- 1 tsp. dried thyme
- 1 tsp. ground cumin
- ½ tsp. onion powder
- ½ tsp. garlic powder
- 1 tsp. salt
- ¼ tsp. black pepper
- 1 lb. thick skin-on salmon fillets, cut into chunks
- Vegetable oil
- Cherry tomatoes
- 1 red onion, cut into chunks
- Small flour or soft corn tortillas
- Shredded lettuce or cabbage
- Guacamole
- Lime wedges

Mix paprika, cayenne, thyme, cumin, onion powder, garlic powder, salt, and pepper. Push salmon into the mixture to coat all sides well. Rub oil over tomatoes and onion chunks. Alternately thread salmon, tomatoes, and onions onto flat cooking sticks and cook over hot embers until salmon is done, carefully turning once partway through cooking. Meanwhile, char some tortillas over the fire if you'd like. Remove the food from the skewers. Discard the skin from the salmon and flake the meat. Fill the tortillas with the cooked food, lettuce, and guacamole. Squeeze lime juice over the tacos, fold, and eat. Campfire food never tasted so good!

STATE FAIR SMOKED CHOPS

Makes 4 servings **STICK**

Ahead of time, in a big resealable plastic bag, mix brown sugar and honey, vegetable oil, lime juice, and red pepper flakes. Remove the bone from 2 large pork chops and cut the meat in half. Add the meat to the bag, seal, and marinate for at least 20 minutes. Discard the marinade and push each pork chop half onto a sturdy cooking stick. Hold over medium embers until sizzling and heated through, rotating to brown all sides. Eat right off the stick like at the fair or be a little more civilized and use a fork and knife.

INGREDIENTS

- ¼ cup brown sugar
- ¼ cup honey
- 1 tbsp. vegetable oil
- 1 lime, juiced
- 1 tsp. red pepper flakes
- 2 large 1"-thick fully cooked smoked pork chops

TERIYAKI MEATBALL SPEARS

Makes 4–6 servings STICK

Cut fresh pineapple, white onion, and red and green bell pepper into bite-size chunks. Alternately thread the food onto cooking sticks with fully cooked meatballs. Hold over a cooking fire, rotating every few minutes until everything is hot and lightly charred, brushing with warmed apple or apricot jelly the last few minutes.

INGREDIENTS

- 1 fresh pineapple
- 1 white onion
- 1 red bell pepper
- 1 green bell pepper
- 1 (18 oz.) pkg. frozen meatballs, thawed and fully cooked

SAUCES

Do the sandwiches and kebabs in this book
NEED a dipping sauce? Not necessarily. But for a
bit of indulgence, add one to your sandwich before
cooking or dunk your kebab into one after.
Store sauces in the refrigerator for up to 1 or 2 weeks.

CHIPOTLE MAYO

In a blender or food processer, blend ½ cup mayo, ¼ cup sour cream, 2 peppers from a can of chipotles peppers in adobo, and the juice of lime until finely chopped.

CREAMY HONEY MUSTARD

Stir together ¼ cup mayo, 2 tbsps. honey, 1 tbsp. yellow mustard, 1 tbsp. whole grain Dijon mustard, and 2 tbsps. barbecue sauce.

CHIMICHURRI SAUCE

In a blender or food processor, blend ½ cup each fresh parsley, fresh cilantro, olive oil, and red wine vinegar, ¼ cup chopped onion, 3-4 cloves minced garlic, 1 tsp. dried oregano, and ½ tsp. each salt and crushed red pepper until finely chopped.

BLUE & BACON SPREAD

Mix ½ cup mayo, ¼ c crumbled blue cheese, and 2 crisp-cooked bacon slices (crumbled).

WASABI SAUCE

Stir together ½ cup mayo, 1 tbsp. prepared hot wasabi, 1 tbsp. lime juice, and 1 tbsp. chopped cilantro.

HERBY OIL & VINEGAR

In a lidded jar, combine ¾ cup olive oil, ¼ cup red wine vinegar, 1 tsp. dried basil, 1 tsp. dried oregano, ¼ tsp. salt, and ¼ tsp. black pepper. Shake.

DESSERTS

Who says sandwiches and kebabs are just for savory foods? So many sweets await you–end your day with a treat as the moon rises and the crickets chirp.

STRAWBERRY CHEESECAKE SANDWICH

Makes 1 sandwich per 2 bread slices  **PIE IRON**

INGREDIENTS

- 2 slices of white bed, one side buttered
- 2 tbsps. cream cheese, softened
- 1 tbsp. strawberry jam
- 2 strawberries, sliced
- ¼ tsp. honey
- ⅛ tsp. fresh mint

Spread the cream cheese and jam on the unbuttered side of the bread. Layer remaining ingredients between slices and toast both sides.

SWEET CINNAMON SANDWICH

Makes 1 sandwich per 2 bread slices  **PIE IRON**

INGREDIENTS

- 2 cinnamon raisin bread slices, one side buttered
- 2 tbsps. mascarpone
- ½ cup blueberries
- ½ cup semisweet chocolate chips

Spread mascarpone on the unbuttered side of the bread. Layer remaining ingredients between bread slices and toast both sides.

BANANA BREAD DESSERT SANDWICH

Makes 1 sandwich per 2 bread slices  **PIE IRON**

Spread the cream cheese, peanut butter, and chocolate hazelnut on the unbuttered side of the bread. Layer remaining ingredients between slices and toast both sides.

INGREDIENTS

- 2 banana bread slices, one side buttered
- 2 tbsps. cream cheese, softened
- 2 tbsps. creamy peanut butter
- 2 tbsps. chocolate hazelnut spread
- 1 banana, sliced
- ⅔ cup mini marshmallows

TOASTED FRUIT & WHITE CHOCOLATE
Servings vary  STICK FOIL

Place white chocolate chips in a small aluminum pan; cover with foil and set near the fire to melt. Stir in vegetable oil and keep warm. Cut pears, bananas, apples, and pineapple into chunks; dip into orange juice and thread onto cooking sticks, alternating with fresh blackberries and regular marshmallows if you'd like. Sprinkle everything with a little cinnamon. Hold over medium-hot embers for a couple of minutes, turning frequently. Dip the fruit into the melted white chocolate for a decadent sweet treat!

INGREDIENTS
- 1 cup white chocolate chips
- 1 tsp. vegetable oil
- 1 fresh pear, sliced
- 1 cup fresh blackberries
- 1 banana, sliced
- 1 apple, sliced
- ½ cup fresh pineapple
- 1 cup orange juice
- ½ cup marshmallows, regular
- Cinnamon, to taste

STRAWBERRY MERINGUE BITES

Servings vary  STICK FOIL

Place chocolate candy wafers in a small aluminum pan; cover with foil and set near the fire to melt. Once melted, dip whole fresh strawberries partway into the chocolate and set upside-down to harden a bit. Dip the berry into marshmallow fluff (or swirl it on using a knife) and push a cooking stick through the stem end. Hold over medium-hot embers, turning as needed until the fluff is nice and toasty.

INGREDIENTS

- 1 cup chocolate candy wafers
- Strawberries
- Marshmallow fluff

BERRY-MALLOW PUFFS

Makes 10 servings **STICK**

Separate biscuits from a 7.5 oz. tube of refrigerated biscuits (10 ct.) and flatten each; sprinkle with cinnamon-sugar. Flatten a regular marshmallow and set it in the center of the biscuit. Add 1 or 2 fresh blackberries or raspberries (cut in half if large) or a few blueberries; sprinkle with a little orange zest. Fold the biscuit around the filling, pressing seams firmly to seal. Insert a cooking fork through the center of the biscuit. Cook slowly over warm embers until brown on the outside and no longer doughy in the center, rotating often to brown evenly.

INGREDIENTS

- 7.5 oz. tube of refrigerated biscuits (10 ct.)
- Cinnamon-sugar, to taste
- Marshmallows, regular
- Blackberries or raspberries or blueberries
- Orange zest

PIÑA COLADA TRES LECHES DESSERT

Makes 6–8 servings **STICK**

In a resealable plastic bag, combine sweetened condensed milk, evaporated milk, coconut milk, ½ tsp. cinnamon, and 2 beaten egg yolks. Seal the bag and shake to blend. Cut about ¾ lb. unsliced French bread into 1" cubes and add them to the bag; seal and turn to coat. Push the coated bread cubes onto cooking sticks alternately with pineapple chunks and hold over warm embers until the bread is no longer "eggy" in the middle. Transfer bread and pineapple to bowls and top with toasted coconut and cherries (and if you have whipped cream, add that too).

INGREDIENTS

- ½ cup sweetened condensed milk
- ½ cup evaporated milk
- ½ cup coconut milk
- ½ tsp. cinnamon
- 2 egg yolks, beaten
- French bread
- Pineapple, cut into chunks
- Toasted coconut
- Cherries
- Whipped cream, optional

CAMPING ECLAIRS

Makes 4 servings **STICK**

INGREDIENTS

- 1 (3.4 oz.) pkg. instant pudding mix (we used French vanilla, but use what you like)
- 1¾ cup milk
- 1 tsp. vanilla or almond extract, optional
- 1 (7.5 oz.) tube refrigerated biscuits (8 ct.)
- Spray whipped cream
- Thick hot fudge sauce or chocolate frosting

Ahead of time, whisk together pudding mix, milk, and extract until smooth. Transfer to a resealable plastic bag; seal and chill until needed.

Cover about 8" at the end of a 1" diameter cooking stick or dowel with foil; grease it well. For each eclair, press two biscuits together and flatten well. Wrap the dough around the foil end of the stick to make a tube about 4" long; pinch edges together tightly to seal.

Hold the stick over warm embers and cook slowly until brown on the outside and no longer doughy in the middle. Carefully slide the biscuit tube off the stick.

Cut off a corner of the bag containing the pudding and pipe pudding into each tube; fill with whipped cream. Top with fudge sauce or frosting and dig in.

COOKING TIP
You can't rush it when cooking dough over the fire, but the time it takes pays off big-time when you take a bite of these eclairs!

S'MORES GALORE

Servings vary  **STICK**

FUNKY MONKEY

Load up a chocolate graham cracker with Nutella, banana slices, and a toasted strawberry marshmallow. Add another cracker and you've got yummy goodness!

CAMPER'S DREAM

Start with a regular graham cracker and smear it with raspberry jam; add dark chocolate pieces and top it off with a toasted marshmallow. Press down with another cracker and be prepared for ooey-gooey deliciousness!

SUNDAE S'MORE

What do you get when you sandwich some cookies & cream candy bar pieces, a toasted marshmallow, and chopped maraschino cherries between two oatmeal cookies? Bliss!

PORK 'N' S'MORE

A basic s'more goes one step further. Toast a marshmallow and layer it between two regular graham crackers along with milk chocolate candy bar squares and crisply cooked bacon.

S'MORE IDEAS

Try these delicious ideas, and you may just find a new favorite s'more.

• **FAUX MINT OREO:** chocolate graham crackers, thin mint candies, toasted marshmallow

• **CINNFULLY HAZELNUT:** cinnamon graham crackers, Nutella, toasted marshmallow

• **CHEESECAKE:** graham crackers, ready-to-eat cheesecake filling, cherry or blueberry pie filling, toasted marshmallow

• **COOKIELICIOUS:** a toasted marshmallow sandwiched between two of your favorite cookies

• **WHITE CHOCOLATE-BERRY:** graham crackers, white chocolate candy pieces, toasted marshmallow, fresh berries

• **PEEPS:** at some point, you've gotta build a s'more with Peeps

PACK ON THE POUND (CAKE)

Makes 1 sandwich per 2 bread slices  **PIE IRON**

INGREDIENTS

- 2 pound cake slices, one side buttered
- 1 dark chocolate bar
- 1 slice brie
- ½ cup raspberries

Layer ingredients between cake slices and toast both sides.

BAKED APPLES

Makes 4 servings **STICK**

INGREDIENTS

- 4 large apples
- ¼ cup sugar
- 1 tsp. cinnamon
- 1 tsp. ground nutmeg
- Whipped cream, optional
- Ice cream, optional
- Marshmallow fluff, optional

Place sugar in a small aluminum pan and stir in a little cinnamon and ground nutmeg (and just a pinch of cayenne pepper if you'd like a surprising little kick); set aside. For each apple, push a sturdy cooking stick into the bottom of your favorite kind of baking apple, about halfway through.

Hold above hot embers, rotating occasionally, until the skin browns and loosens. Pull the apple away from the heat, use a sharp knife to carefully remove the skin, and then roll the apple in the sugar mixture until evenly coated. Eat it right off the stick or slice and serve with whipped cream, ice cream, or marshmallow fluff – whatever you have available. Any way you slice it (or don't), it's wonderful!

CANDY-MALLOW POPPERS

Servings vary  **STICK**

For each popper, first push a marshmallow onto a cooking stick. Then add your favorite mini chocolate candy bar right behind the marshmallow, keeping them as close to the pointed end of the stick as possible. Toast carefully over warm embers (you don't want that delicious candy bar melting into the flames). When the marshmallow is golden brown, slowly slip it over the candy and pull both of them off together. The candy bar sets nicely inside the marshmallow and softens slightly, creating a yummy pop-in-your-mouth treat. Pop carefully – they're piping hot!

INGREDIENTS

- Marshmallows, regular
- Mini chocolate candy bar, any kind

INDEX

Note: Page numbers in **bold** indicate TOC lists of recipes by category.